Flair

RIZZOLI
NEW YORK

New York Paris London Milan

Flair

EXQUISITE INVITATIONS, LUSH FLOWERS, AND GORGEOUS TABLE SETTINGS

JOE NYE

WITH CAITLIN LEFFEL

PHOTOGRAPHY BY EDMUND BARR

ACKNOWLEDGMENTS

I'd like to thank my staff that was kind enough to allow me the time to produce this book. Special thanks to Edie Frère, owner of Landis Gifts and Stationery, and Suzanne Rheinstein and Hollyhock who helped immeasurably on this project. Extra thanks also to Doug Turshen, who designed the book, along with Steve Turner. To Edmund Barr who took the luscious photographs and Caitlin Leffel who helped turn my words into something I think people will be interested in reading. To Sandy Gilbert and Ellen Cohen at Rizzoli for their editorial help and guidance. To Pam Sommers who helped me launch this idea and also to Doug Woods for helping to create the idea.

Lastly I'd like to thank my family for their support.

TABLE OF CONTENTS

INTRODUCTION 9

INTRODUCTION

I inherited my passion for entertaining from my mother. I grew up in rural Nebraska—literally in the middle of nowhere—yet my parents managed to carve out a pretty sophisticated lifestyle for themselves. Each month, they hosted a black-tie dinner party, for which my mother cooked a beautiful meal—on her own, without any help. She bought fresh, seasonal flowers, which she arranged simply, but neatly. The table was set with one of her many collections of china, silver, and freshly ironed linen tablecloths and napkins. Nothing was showy—just elegant and comfortable. Generally, cocktails and hors d'oeuvres were served first, then guests sat down to dinner, and afterwards, there was card-playing, and sometimes even some dancing. What is remarkable about this as I recall it now is how natural it was for my mother to do all of the cooking, the flower arranging, setting the table by herself. Having guests in her home for these long, fun-filled evenings was something she enjoyed—it wasn't a chore, and she embraced it. She was confident in her skills and excelled at creating an environment that was elegant, unfussy, and welcoming.

These days, we live in a world where perfect-looking, ready-made, pre-packaged items of convenience are much more readily available than they were when my mother was planning her parties. This has created an environment that has led many people to think that they can't accomplish these tasks—arrange flowers, host a sit-down dinner—themselves. But they can. What my mother taught me is that you don't necessarily have to do anything fancy or complicated to throw a successful gathering. I believe that anyone can entertain well, if they do it stylishly. With common sense, some basic knowledge, and a playful spirit, you can create a welcoming atmosphere that's more impressive than one you can buy pre-packaged in a store.

This is not to say that I'm preaching nostalgia. I have used pre-printed invitations, ordered stamps online, served guests dinner out of my kitchen, and often bought flowers at the grocery store. Great hosts usually blend hands-on work with a few well-chosen short cuts and quick fixes. I compare it to being an orchestra conductor. You know what concert you are planning to perform, and have a certain amount of instruments that you control. At some types of gatherings, you'll focus on certain elements, while others take a supporting role; other times, something that was in chorus steals the spotlight. Not everything has to be—or should be—commanding the focus all the time. There can only be so many stars of the show.

Another thing I admired about my mother's entertaining style was her smart attention to detail. As a guest, I find it's the gestures rooted in common sense that really impress me: an ironed tablecloth brushed free of crumbs; a custom stamp on an invitation, a vase that has been wiped free of condensation. None of these things takes long to do, or is very complicated—they're just thoughtful and make your guests feel like you've considered everything.

As a host, it's easy to forget that "thoughtful" and "lovely" aren't the same as "perfect." I've seen flowers presented in water pitchers, soup served out of coffee cups, and admired plenty of hand-written, filled-in invitations. As long as each gesture is done neatly and thoughtfully, I believe it's fine—often even better—if not everything matches, isn't fancy or expensive, and doesn't look as perfect as a display in a store. Casual *is* elegant, as long it's not sloppy.

I wrote this book because I truly enjoy planning and hosting parties, not because I want to teach people how to do it "right." I love every aspect of entertaining: creating a guest list and a party style, matching details to an occasion, choosing colors and decorative elements. And then there's the "research"—entertaining is a wonderful excuse to spend some time in stationery stores, florist shops and flowers markets, and little boutiques that sell tableware, candles, and bibelots for your table. Though you can go online to find these, if you have the time, visiting shops is one of the best ways to get creative inspiration and ideas, and these shopping trips can be one of the most inspirational parts of the experience for you as the host. I always look forward to brainstorming clever invitation ideas at my local stationer and chatting with favorite vendors at the flower market to find out which flowers are best for my occasion.

Over the years, I have orchestrated or helped plan countless wonderful, memorable gatherings of all shapes, sizes, and styles. But there's one evening that always stands out in my mind. When I was eighteen years old, one of my sisters was getting married and wanted to have her wedding at our home. At the time, I was working for some friends of my parents who owned a floral shop (where I learned many tricks I still use today), and I helped my mother with the decorating. It was the middle of March, with ten feet of snow on the ground, and we decided to create a spring extravaganza. We imported anemones, lilacs, calendulas, tulips—we ordered every spring flower that we could think of delivered to this tiny town in the middle of Nebraska. The profusion of flowers and the colors— shades of red, pink, orange, violet, and bright yellows—just came alive. Because it was a March wedding, we also served spring food—asparagus, lamb—and though the actual day was freezing, our early Easter buffet was a perfect complement to the flowers. We took out every linen napkin that my mother had and set the buffet table with a pink tablecloth that she had a seamstress make. My three sisters wore yellow dresses, which contrasted beautifully with our floral arrangements. We did everything ourselves, it wasn't perfect, not everything matched, and yet I still think of this as one of the loveliest parties I have ever attended. When I'm feeling overwhelmed by the amount of work and planning I have to do for a gathering, I think of my sister's wedding party to remind myself of how the most wonderful events are not always the most lavish, the ones with the best food, or most expensive flowers. They are the ones where the host has put in some care and creativity, and so obviously enjoyed everything from the first minute of planning until the very last guest has gone home.

TABLE SETTINGS

TABLE SETTING AND TABLE DECOR

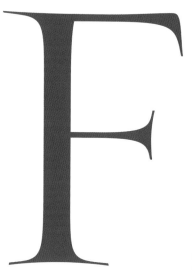

lowers and invitations are generally things that you buy or create for a specific gathering. With table settings and table decor, however, it is more likely that you will be working with pieces you already have. Everyone has their own particular collection of tableware and serving dishes: pieces that they've inherited, been given, or accumulated over the years. Your own particular mix— no matter what it is or how much of it you have—can be used at any number of occasions over and over again. No matter what you own, you can always work with it. So don't fight it!

Out of the client's extensive collection of china, crystal, and silver, and right in the middle of prime rose-growing season.

SETTING THE TABLE

Setting a table is a lot like getting dressed. You put on the essentials first (the tablecloth or placemats), then you pull together an "outfit" based on what you are doing that day (china with a colorful pattern for a ladies' lunch or bamboo plates for a meal outside). Finally, you add "accessories" that go with what you've already got on (placecard holders, finger bowls, charger plates, and crystal). Getting into these extra elements can be fun, and just as you can wear your grandmother's good jade brooch on a regular day, so, from time to time, can you throw these once strictly formal pieces onto a more casual table. Just remember to keep the entire ensemble in mind, and don't forget what type of gathering you're getting the table dressed for.

The only hard-and-fast requirements for setting a table are that you need something to put the food and drinks on or in, something to serve them out of, and something with which to serve them. Within those three "somethings" are dozens of items that you can customize based on the nature of the event and what you own. If you are serving a soup course, for instance, don't worry if you don't have enough (or any!) soup bowls. You don't need soup bowls to serve soup. You can serve it in coffee mugs, cereal bowls, tumblers, or even hollowed-out squashes. An unexpected touch on the table underscores the lighthearted tone at casual gatherings and will add a compelling element of contrast at formal parties.

When you are hosting in your home, it's inevitable that not everything will match. And I think this is a good thing! Your gathering should

Black bamboo flatware from Juliska adds an unexpected note when mixed with a chinoiserie-style tablecloth and pink carnations.

Pink carnations are a favorite of mine and absolutely effortless to
arrange in silver mint julep cups as individual centerpieces. Handmade
chargers in the Palladian pattern are from Isis Ceramics Ltd.

A profusion of pink carnations makes a powerful color statement in this chinoiserie-themed party. Black accents create drama and sophistication.

have a different look than one held in a restaurant or banquet hall. Rather than try to cover up mismatching items, make the mix a part of your decor. When you are setting the table, think about contrast (for instance, if you have two different types of china, alternate one place setting with the other, or mix the pieces within each place setting); the type of gathering you are having (formal or casual, sit-down or buffet); and what you'll be serving. My rule is to match every fussy gesture with a plain one. So if you are using china with an ornate floral pattern and gold edges, choose serving pieces that are plain white or a solid color.

There are ways to decorate a table beyond a single, floral centerpiece and other traditional elements (candles, for instance) to achieve a desired effect. For an evening buffet, there is nothing as magical as one principal floral arrangement in the center of the table and several smaller ones elsewhere around the table. Then scatter votive candles in clear cylindrical cups around the food. For a sit-down dinner, fill all of the water glasses to the brim with ice, and again, place tons of votive candles around the food and the flowers. The light shining up from the votives will make the water glasses twinkle as well as illuminate the flowers and food in a very flattering way ... and it will make your guests feel great, too, because everyone looks better in candlelight!

Another way to add some life to your table settings is to incorporate whimsical touches with decorative items from an arts and crafts store. Recently in one such shop, for instance, I found some inexpensive butterfly and bird ornaments that would look fabulous suspended from a chandelier with fishing line, or attached to a manzanita branch for an Easter egg tree. Five-and-dime stores, which used to be great places to buy these little sundries, are sadly, mostly obsolete.

Mottahedeh dessert plates mixed with Charlotte Moss's treillage-patterned plates make for a fresh, summery dinner party.

I always encourage clients to mix periods and styles of dining chairs so that the dining room doesn't look static. Tall, swirly hurricanes in a gorgeous amethyst color from William Yeoward bring out the aubergine color in the dinnerware and curtains, and coordinate with the amethyst goblets.

The sideboard is set with the
makings of the dinner table.
A vase of simple calla lilies
provides an unexpected flourish.
Opposite: Mottahedeh
demitasse cups and saucers.

DISHWARE

Many good sets of china have busy or old-fashioned patterns. When people are given a set like this, these outdated patterns may make them reluctant to use it. This is a shame; if you've got something like that, don't be afraid of it! If your china has an intricate pattern—flowers, for instance—try picking a color from within the pattern and letting that guide your choices for the centerpiece, table linens, invitations, and other party decor. Or incorporate solid-colored pieces, such as bowls or salad plates, within each place setting to break up the pattern a bit.

On the other hand, china in a simple, modern pattern, or dishware in solid colors will lend a starker feel to a table. Both typically convey a chic, more formal look, but this can be tempered by an injection of color in the other table decor. If you are working on a registry or just starting to build your dishware collection, stick with a single color palette and a simple pattern. This will be the easiest to work with, and their versatility will come in handy if you inherit or are given something with a more complicated pattern.

A mélange of blue-and-white ceramics mixed with yellow gladioli and oncidium orchids creates a fun juxtaposition to this very modern kitchen. The painting in the background is by Eric Johnson.

Blue and yellow creates an exciting color scheme that is both classic and spirited. A single yellow Fuji mum in a teacup makes for a fast, simple individual centerpiece. The Torquay dinnerware is from Mottahedeh.

Bright yellow button mums and Fuji mums make
an interesting and colorful combination.

Right: Shopping for antique blue-and-white porcelain at Hollyhock. *Below:* At Crate and Barrel, I am arranging a possibility of blue glassware, white porcelain, and blue-and-white porcelain on a striped placement.

Opposite: A remarkable chinoiserie tea table provides a striking backdrop for an antique coffee service and blue linen cocktail napkins.

FLATWARE

Ideally, I suggest having several sets of flatware so that you can vary what you use according to the type of party you're having. You can also try mixing pieces from different sets. If having multiple sets doesn't suit your budget or storage capabilities, you'll want the simplest design you can find so it can be used at any gathering. At the types of stores listed on the previous page, you can also find interesting flatware, often quite inexpensively, to supplement your collection. For formal gatherings, silver is traditional and lovely, but it's not the end of the world if you don't have it. Stainless-steel utensils are now offered in the same elegant patterns as silver, and they are dishwasher-safe.

(But though I'm usually a big proponent of mixing, I draw the line here. Never use silver and stainless steel together.)

It used to be fashionable and proper to have specific utensils for every type of food. This custom has long since become obsolete, but these specialized items can be fun to see on a table nonetheless. You can use fish forks for a salad course at a dinner, while fruit forks and knives look appropriately dainty at a tea. Consignment shops are great places to find eccentric little items such as these.

A beautiful example of sterling-silver flatware in an unusual pattern.

This dream client actually let me have flatware handmade from James
Robinson Inc., in New York. Water goblets and green wineglasses are
from William Yeoward. An antique set of Coalport is used for serving.

To go with the Duke of Gloucester dinnerware, I mixed bright orange ranunculus, parrot tulips, geranium leaves, and berries into lovely bouquets. Solid orange and green William Yeoward china is paired with antique Imari serving pieces and Lunt trellis flatware.

GLASSWARE

Drinking wine from stemless glasses has become very popular, so if you have a set of these, you can actually use the same glasses for wine, water, and even mixed drinks. You can find them everywhere now. I like the paper-thin tumblers from Martha Stewart. They come in different colors, which can be a nice touch depending on the type of gathering you're having and theme. Colored glass looks especially lovely when mixed with classic lead crystal.

If you are serving a specialty cocktail—such as flavored martinis, margaritas, or mint juleps at a Kentucky Derby party—consider investing in special glasses for it. These can be found rather inexpensively at stores such as Cost Plus World Market or Pier 1 Imports, but the visual touch of these notable shapes in guests' hands will make the drinks—and the theme of the party—nicely pronounced.

People sometimes get hung up on the proper way to place the flatware and glasses on the table, and it's easy to see why. There is official protocol for just about any possible meal. (The original *Joy of Cooking* has wonderful illustrations of many of these, but the details can be overwhelming!) You don't need to memorize all of the rules to set your table, you just need common sense: Arrange the silverware and glassware, from left to right (on the left side) or right to left (on the right side), in the order that it will be used. (There are a lot of nuances for serving and clearing as well, but all you really need to know is to serve from the left, clear from the right, and when you are clearing, not to stack the plates on top of each other like a busboy in a diner!)

This beautifully etched crystal is vintage Orrefors. Its diminutive size and pattern make it interesting.

Contemporary Chinese Chippendale
chargers marry beautifully with
antique china and aqua finger bowls.

Vintage red tumblers add a shot of color to very traditional dinnerware.
Oatmeal-colored linen napkins, woven placemats, Wedgwood, and
a favorite Spode pattern make for a great casual lunch table setting.

SILVER

Whether inherited or discovered at a flea market, old or new silver distinguishes a table like nothing else. I love the wonderful glint that it lends to a table setting, like a glimmer of anticipation for the meal to come.

Most people have at least a few pieces of silver, whether a full set of flatware (knives, forks, and spoons), several pieces of hollowware (serving bowls, pitchers, creamers, and sugar bowls), or a little of both. But so many people keep "the good silver" hidden away and only drag it out on Christmas and Thanksgiving. I'm of the opinion that if you own it, it's silly to deprive yourself of its loveliness 363 days a year. Of course, you may want to save the full regalia—flatware plus hollowware—for those special occasions. But in small doses, silver adds a little glamour to everyday living. An additional incentive: Silver used regularly doesn't need to be polished as often.

There are several types of silver. Sterling silver is nearly solid silver. Silver plate is when the silver is fused to some other metal. Sheffield plate is my favorite because the silver has been fused to copper, and over time, the copper wears through, which I think is a lovely effect—one similar to aging gracefully.

If you inherit or are given silver, you'll likely receive a complete set in a matching pattern. When buying from thrift stores or flea markets, of course, this is not always the case. Either way, don't be afraid to mix things up. Pair fancy and ornate pieces with simpler ones, and break everything up with shots of color. A mélange of styles and patterns is something everyone at your table will enjoy!

From a client's extraordinary collection of antique silver, three pieces at different heights make for a stunning tablescape.

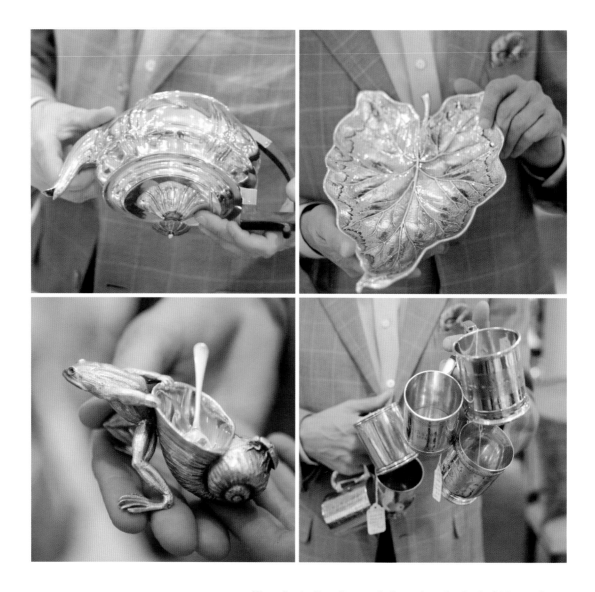

There is sterling silver and silver plate, both of which are shown here. *Opposite:* An antique Regency candlestick inside an etched-glass hurricane is set against silk-damask wall upholstery.

PLACEMATS AND TABLECLOTHS

Placemats come in a variety of materials, and they don't have to be relegated to kids' birthday parties and family dinners. If you have a nice table, using placemats is actually a great way to show it off. Placemats can be plastic, wicker, rattan, paper, wood, and of course, linen. Linen placemats are generally considered the most formal. Obviously, they require a little bit more upkeep in terms of washing and ironing, but they make a chic accent under a placesetting. One way to incorporate placemats at a buffet is to give guests their place settings on trays lined with paper or linen placemats.

Conversely, tablecloths don't necessarily have to be reserved for fancy dinner parties, and if you don't have a pretty table, a great tablecloth is a way to camouflage it. A woman I know, who frequently entertains outdoors, has a fabulous collection of bright, cotton terrycloth tablecloths

that she had made very inexpensively, and they're wonderful because they don't require any ironing or special laundering. She can simply throw them into the wash after the pool party or lunch is over. And I think simply covering the table with newspaper is a fun (and practical) touch at a clambake. But resist the temptation to use plastic or vinyl tablecloths (*ever*), and when you are using a linen one, make sure to press it first. An easy way to do this is to iron it right on the table, with a layer of padding underneath.

If you have a few tablecloths, make sure to have one that's pure white—it goes with everything. Like a painter's canvas, a white tablecloth provides a neutral starting point on which to illustrate the tone of your party.

White linens are a must-have for entertaining. They provide a crisp backdrop for any kind of patterned dinnerware. Fresh garden roses are the perfect complement.

For a fun Mexican lunch, brightly striped placemats and yellow bowls from the hardware store mix nicely with a set of chrome Milo Baughman dining chairs. Hot mixes of strongly colored flowers set the tone for a festive party.

NAPKINS

Napkins are, I think, the most important element of the table setting. They have a crucial function—keeping the food in your mouth and not in your lap (or someone else's for that matter)—and they don't blend in. They are a way to add color to a table, don't take up much storage space, and are relatively simple to acquire; plus they are more easily varied than dishware, flatware, and glassware. I am a big proponent of using cloth napkins for all occasions—even cocktail parties. Cloth napkins acquired a bad rap as the convenience of the disposable varieties took hold, but perhaps now that conservation has come into favor, paper napkins will seem unfashionably wasteful, and cloth napkins will come back into vogue. Regardless of what fashion dictates, cloth napkins are one of those *soigné* gestures that kicks any party—even the most casual—up a notch. You can get them very, very inexpensively these days, and the added maintenance (ironing is a must) is worth the time. There are plenty of other places where you can cut corners.

If you only want to own one or two sets of cloth napkins, I recommend they be somewhere between 22 by 22 and 27 by 27 inches square, because then they can be used for all settings: luncheons, sit-down dinners, or buffets. You want to avoid tiny napkins when you are serving a meal because they just won't do the job. This is especially important at buffets, where people are moving around with food in their hands and possibly balancing plates on their laps. You don't want your guests to end up wearing the shrimp Creole you're serving!

Twenty-seven-inch square, white, hem-stitched dinner napkins go with everything and are large enough to cover your lap for a buffet-style meal.

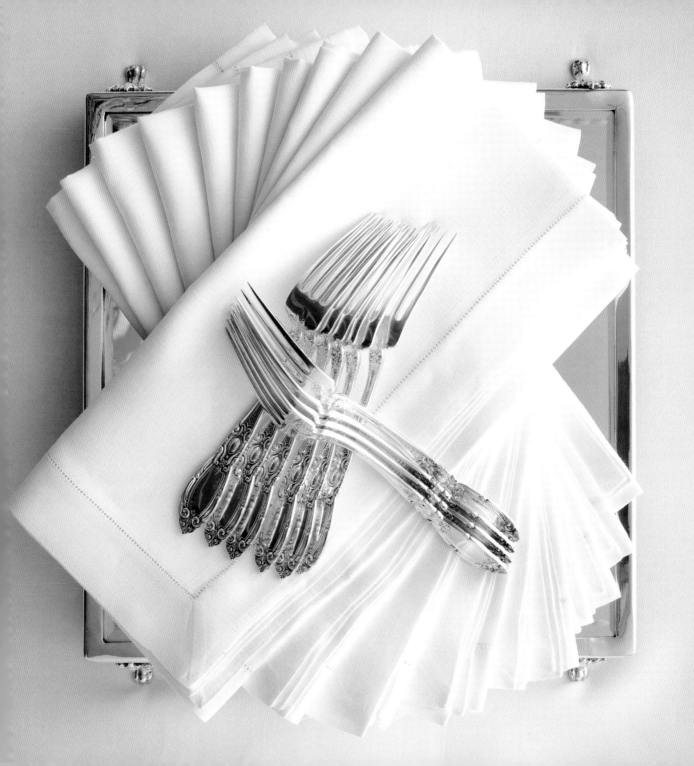

I love wonderful old damask or linen napkins, which often can be found at estate sales or consignment shops. They are usually oversize and so wonderful for buffets, picnics, and outdoor entertaining since they will cover up your whole lap. They frequently will have monograms on them—monograms that are not your own—and that is absolutely okay. It's an unexpected, slightly off-kilter touch that will give your table decor personality (even if the "personality" is borrowed from someone else!).

At a cocktail party, you should have enough napkins so that guests will be able to take a new one each time they get a new drink plus extras for the hors d'oeuvres. I like to estimate four to six napkins per guest. If you are using cloth napkins, and that sounds like an overwhelming amount of laundering and ironing, you can start out with cloth napkins (estimating about two per guest) and switch to paper napkins as the evening goes by.

If you do decide to use paper napkins at a cocktail party (with—or in lieu of—cloth napkins), choose them wisely. There are many different kinds of paper cocktail napkins, both in solid colors and in prints, and there are some very attractive ones available now. But when choosing paper napkins, you should pay the most attention to the quality of the paper. You want to make sure that you get something that feels nice and smooth on the face, and that is adequately absorbent for messy finger food. If you're going to go with paper napkins, buy the highest quality ones you can find.

Below: **Beautiful embroidered linen cocktail napkins from Nancy Stanley Waud come in all colors and styles.**

Above: **Try to provide several different sets of cocktail napkins, and in abundance, since each guest will use at least three or four for drinks and food.**

Red, printed silk-toile tablecloths, and blue and red
glassware from Cost Plus World Market mix wonderfully
with fancy sterling silver and Blue Canton dinner plates.

A stunning dining room lined in Gracie wallpaper with beautiful antique Derby dinnerware.

The much-maligned gypsophila (commonly known as baby's breath), when used alone and in profusion, makes a pretty counterpoint to the formality of the room.

TIPS FOR ELEGANT TABLE SETTING

Make sure your table is perfectly, spotlessly clean. The flowers, the decoration, and the mood will be overshadowed by breadcrumbs from the morning's breakfast on the table.

■ *Check that every part of the place setting—from the flatware to the plates and the stemware—is in perfect alignment and that the spaces between settings and from settings to the edge of the table are even. You may even want to go so far as to use a tape measure to check that all of the spacing is identical, as they do at the White House.*

■ *Thoroughly wipe the containers in which you are displaying your flowers before placing them on the table, to prevent water on the exteriors from dripping onto your tablecloth or staining your table.*

■ *After the table is set, wipe everything down with a damp cloth. Setting the table a day in advance is a great way to maximize your time the day of your party, but if you do this, cover everything up with a clean sheet until right before the guests arrive.*

■ *Never put a coffee cup and saucer by a first-course place setting. Always bring them out afterward.*

Uniquities, my favorite consignment shop, has beautiful treasures from the plain to fancy.

BUFFETS AND COCKTAIL PARTIES

Buffets are nice because they allow your guests to control the amount of food they take, and they can be a useful format if you're having more guests than you can seat around your dinner table. Buffets can be more casual than sit-down meals, but they don't have to be—you can use flowers and other decorative elements to convey a more elegant tone.

There are a couple of options for presenting and serving your meal when you are hosting a buffet. When choosing, you'll want to think most about what works best for your space and the equipment you have (such as serving pieces and tableware). The most basic way to set up is to place the dishes, napkins, and utensils at one end of the buffet table, and have guests serve themselves. Once they've gone through the line, they can either take their plates to another table or to chairs and sofas, where they will eat from their laps.

If your buffet table is short on space or you want to organize who will sit where, another way to set up the service is to have guests serve themselves from the buffet table, and then bring their plates back to a table that is set with the silverware, glasses, and place cards, if you are using them. The plates can either be stacked at the buffet table, or placed on the table like regular place settings for guests to retrieve first.

Tray meals—where guests pick up a tray with their place setting on it—are a nice, organized-looking option for when you won't be seating guests at tables or for outdoor meals. Another service idea for a casual, intimate gathering is to serve your guests from the kitchen. This works particularly well for meals that are served from a

French ceramic dinnerware from Hollyhock mixes beautifully for an inside/outside summer party.

Dessert is served in Dodie Thayer green-lettuce ware. Red gladioli epitomize summer and are dramatic as a centerpiece on the table.

Wicker trays are a stylish way to serve a casual meal.

single pot, such as winter stews or pasta, and when you have nice-looking cookware. (Pyrex bowls, Le Creuset pots, and brightly colored mixing bowls are all very chic.) You may have more guests at a buffet than place settings, so in this situation, you should really consider mixing pieces. Contrasting charger plates, for instance, can be set out alongside regular dinner plates, adding a nice visual touch.

Self-service is the common feature of all buffets, and it can be hard for guests to gracefully serve themselves while balancing plates on the table edge and carrying on a conversation. You can alleviate this awkwardness by making sure that the serving utensils are well suited to the dish in which they are put. Make sure serving spoons for vegetables and side dishes are amply large, the knife to cut the meat is sharp and dishes that need forks don't have spoons, and vice versa. This will also help to speed up the buffet line, which all of your guests will appreciate.

One final thing to remember about buffets: The food is, literally, the focus. So while you may rid yourself of having to set a table by serving a meal buffet-style, pay attention to presentation on the buffet table. If the food itself is a knockout, consider serving everything out of simple, plain white serving bowls and platters. This choice could drive a black-and-white theme, or, if you want an extra visual touch, use bright, solid-color plates. If your food isn't as photogenic, camouflage it with brighter, busier platters and bowls.

Cocktail parties are the most forgiving form of entertaining, and because guests don't take in all the dining elements at the same time, they are a good place to start if you are nervous about mixing mismatched pieces or having to call upon pieces to perform non-traditional functions (such as using coffee saucers for hors d'oeuvres plates).

Be sure to have plenty of glasses and napkins as well as any other pieces that are particular to the food you're serving.

STOCKING AND SETTING UP THE BAR

A classic drinks tray allows your guests to fix their drinks just the way they like them.

■ Most of us aren't lucky enough to maintain a lifestyle that calls for a permanent, full bar setup in the corner of the living room. So when you are throwing a party, you'll need to stock up on certain beverages. I suggest deciding what to offer and then buying the most expensive variety of it that you can afford.

■ A basic full bar should include a mixture of dark and light liquors, beer, and wine (at least one white and one red). Scotch, bourbon, gin, vodka, and sweet and dry vermouth will cover pretty much any drink a guest could think up. Tonic water, ginger ale, cranberry juice, and another tangy juice are good to have on hand as mixers.

Some people also like to stock sodas, such as Coca-Cola and 7UP. And always keep a good supply of flat and sparkling water for those who prefer not to drink.

■ If all of this sounds too fussy, you can forgo the mixed drinks and just serve beer and wine. That's certainly more economical, and if the party is quite casual, it's perfectly fine not to go all out. Or you can choose to serve one type of cocktail or alcoholic beverage along with beer and wine. If your gathering has a theme, you may want to come up with a drink that goes along with it (such as piña coladas for a beach party or mojitos for a Cinco de Mayo celebration) or one that goes with the color scheme or aesthetic you've established.

PAPER

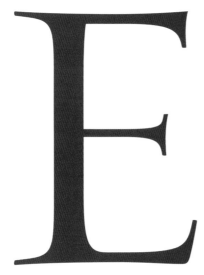

Every party begins with an invitation. A paper invitation is also something guests can save, to remind them of the event after it is over. Invitations are part of the experience that the host provides for his or her guests, but they also offer some of the most fun and creative choices in the planning process. From choosing the type of invitation (custom, preprinted, or handwritten) to drafting the wording to coming up with unique decorative touches for the card and the envelope, there is a wealth of possibilities from which to draw to make each invitation you send special and memorable.

If you choose, you can incorporate related paper elements—in the form of place cards, menu cards, and favors for guests to take home—into your gathering. Each of these souvenirs is functional as well as decorative, so as such, should be something that both does its job and fits with the spirit of the gathering.

The paper elements are the most tangible aspects of a party. Give them some thought, and your guests will come away feeling charmed and well cared for.

Splurge and hire a calligrapher to create seriously chic invitations. When your guests receive invitations that look like this one, they will know the occasion is going to be special.

TIMING

Because they are used well before the party starts, invitations are the first things you should think about after you've decided when and what the party is going to be. I like to mail invitations to a holiday or Saturday gathering at least six weeks in advance, and I ask guests to RSVP at least two weeks before the event occurs. If you decide to have your invitations engraved or printed by letterpress, you will need to allow an additional three to six weeks for the printing after you've settled on the design.

The RSVP is a real issue these days. Where I live, many invitees don't respond at all, and sometimes, if they have responded that they are not coming, they'll show up anyway! An exasperating breach of etiquette, but one about which there's little a host can do besides being (gracefully) prepared. Including an "RSVP by" date on the invitation does help mitigate this problem—people tend to be more responsive to a specific date. For my largest gatherings—when my office hosts a cocktail party for three hundred people—we follow up the invitation with an email a day or two before the event as a reminder to guests. The email reminder is not appropriate for all gatherings; I use it only for the most casual functions or for large work-related events.

Charming floral invitations add real femininity to a tea party. Socially acceptable, pretty paper napkins add a nice touch to this floral tea set.

Please come for
Tea
Saturday, July 10
4 o'clock
9239 Doheny Road
Joe Nye
310-550-7557

SHOPPING AND SOURCING

When you are planning your invitation, think about your taste and what you like—then put all of that to the side and open your mind. Let the particulars of the party drive your choices, and give your personal taste veto power. What might seem gauche or unfashionable at first glance may, when used in combination with other contrasting details, be unexpectedly elegant. Also, many classic aspects of invitation design have possibilities beyond the familiar. For instance, while calligraphy may seem too fussy for you to consider, a different kind of hand-lettering can be a way to achieve a chic handwritten look without having to write the invitations yourself. By keeping an open mind, you won't miss the creative possibilities inherent in the traditions you thought you knew, and you'll be able to come up with a personal and fitting invitation every time you host a gathering.

Stationery stores are wonderful sources of inspiration. When I start to plan a party, I visit my favorite local store to pore over preprinted cards and books of samples and talk to people who work in the store about what the party will be like. At a proper stationery store, you can usually find someone who will brainstorm ideas with you and help you come up with the perfect, custom treatment for your invitation. You'll feel the weight of different papers, the quality of the finishes (plain or grainy), and what each finish is like to write on. This process is a very tactile one. While it's possible to order invitations online, I always recommend taking a little time to visit a stationer. It would be an unpleasant surprise to find that ink smudges easily on a paper you've ordered online.

Depending upon the occasion, there are dozens of styles of invitations out there—from fun and snappy to rich and elegant. Make sure the invitations you select follow the theme and tone of the party you're giving.

YOU'RE INVITED

TO JOIN US FOR DINNER
SATURDAY, THE NINETEENTH OF JULY
TWO THOUSAND EIGHT
AT SEVEN O'CLOCK IN THE EVENING
THE WADE HOME
135 SAND POINT ROAD
BAR HARBOR, MAINE

CASUAL ATTIRE

Dinner
for Ginger and Blake
Saturday, September 20th
at 7:30 pm
135 Preston Court
Los Angeles

To Remind

Black Tie

Ginger and Blake

■ *Engraved or letterpress: Engraving is my favorite! It's old-fashioned and is reserved for special events, such as a wedding, a landmark birthday, or a party honoring someone. You can literally feel the difference when you hold it. The same goes for letterpress. One's preference is simply a matter of taste. Letterpress is fashionable right now, whereas I think engraving has a more timeless look.*

■ *Thermography: Sometimes considered the poor man's engraving, thermography is a type of printing in which the ink is raised above the surface of the paper. I'm not a big fan. I think that if you have to resort to thermography, you should just go with flat printing, which is* not as expensive and looks less like you are trying to fake something pricier. But if you are planning something very festive—such as a luau, a Mexican fiesta, or a similar soiree—thermography's shiny look can be a nice splashy touch.

■ *Flat printing: Flat printing is just that—flat. There is no relief or texture to it. I like it for informal gatherings because it translates well into any color or font. For an informal bridal shower I threw for my niece, I used a snappy, multicolored striped card and did flat ink in a bright parrot green on the inside. Because it was a very casual luncheon, I didn't want the invitation to look pretentious just light and to the point.*

■ *The alternatives to traditional custom-printed invitations generally feel less formal, but they don't have to be any less special. You can customize a simple package of preprinted invitation cards, for example, by hiring a letterer to fill them in for you in a distinctive script. Or simply ask a friend with lovely handwriting for a favor. (This is a great option if you have illegible handwriting, as I do!)*

■ *Blank cards are another alternative. Their simplicity gives them a casual elegance, and the absence of a design draws the attention to the details of the card itself. A thick paper stock, a scalloped edge, or a contrasting border may convey more about the spirit of your gathering than a stock illustration would.*

Little packages in fuchsia ribbon complement the singerie-inspired invitations.

Invitations don't have to be complicated. Thick, white card stock, a red Sharpie, and some simple penmanship can make for a glorious and well-noticed invitation.

■ *Get packs of blank cards with lovely images on the front from a museum store.*

■ *Buy a bunch of art or photography postcards from a street vendor.*

■ *Put a plain, solid-colored circle or square sticker on a blank card in a contrasting color.*

■ *Have an artist friend draw something you can scan into your computer and print out.*

■ *One of the greatest invitations I ever did was for a party when time was really tight and I had to get an invitation out "yesterday." I bought a red Sharpie, simply wrote the invitation out in the largest handwriting I could conjure, and* then had Kinko's make copies on thick, 8 by 11-inch card stock. I packaged my cards in plain white mailing envelopes, wrote the addresses in red, put great stamps on the envelopes, and the invitations were out the door!

■ *A note on design: A design that calls attention to itself—one with lots of pictures and graphics, and several different fonts—can work nicely for events that have a lot of personality, such as a themed party, a child's birthday party, or a holiday gathering. But remember that an intricate design isn't necessarily more formal—or more casual. And if your text is straightforward, you may not need to illustrate the purpose of the gathering visually. Less is often more.*

Karen and David Miller
19654 Arden Avenue
Los Angeles, California 90069

Sharpie

Honoring
Melissa and Michael Anderson
Cocktails
and
Buffet Supper
Friday, the tenth of June
six-thirty
at the home of
Joe Nye

310.550.7557

Rsvp

WORDING

Ironically, the part of creating an invitation that many people find the most challenging is figuring out what to say. I've seen hosts get so caught up in finding a fresh way to say "Will you come?" that they go overboard, or worse, forget to include important information such as the date or time! A smoother approach is to lay out the basics first: the date, the time, the address, the dress code (if you are setting one), and the RSVP details. Once you've got those written out, then consider the specifics: Is the gathering an open house that will last for several hours or do you want people to arrive at a certain time? Will you be serving a full meal or just cocktails and hors d'oeuvres? Will there be a speech or ceremony happening at a specific hour? Should guests bring something, or would you like to tell them not to bring anything as in the case of a birthday party where the honoree requests not to receive gifts. (While I personally find that "No gifts please" looks rather gauche, these days many people are embarrassed about receiving presents, so an indication of this on the invitation may be necessary.) Make sure that these details are conveyed gently, but clearly. Then add a simple line that does the actual inviting, such as "Please join us" or "Please come for," or find another way to introduce the details that expresses the mood or purpose of the party. For instance, if you are hosting a birthday party or a tea with a guest of honor, the first line can simply read "Honoring," the second line can provide the guest of honor's name, and then the following lines can give the details, such as the date, time, and location. Either way, your opening line shouldn't divert attention from the most important information.

Please join me
in celebrating
Marisa's Birthday
Saturday April 15th
12 Noon

At My House

with love,
Joe

■ *The way the envelope looks reflects the effort one puts into a party so don't let it be an afterthought. The envelope is eye candy in the mail, and it introduces the party to your guests. This isn't to say that you always need to hire a professional calligrapher to address your envelopes, just that there's a difference between "breezy" and "sloppy." Think of the envelope as part of the invitation, not separate from it, and give it the same amount of consideration you have to what's inside.*

■ *Printed address labels are not my favorite, and I use them only as a last, last resort—even the most expensive ones are still adhesive labels. In a pile of mail, a handwritten address on an envelope always looks more special. If you must use a label, try doing something colorful and a little unusual instead of the ordinary rectangular label with black type. Round stickers with the address and return address information is a fun idea. Another nice alternative to regular return-address labels is to buy an embosser with your name and address on it and use it on the top flap of the back of the envelope. (I always put the return address on the back. It looks much chicer there than it does on the front, upper left-hand corner!)*

■ *The stamp is part of the package and so also something to consider. The post office makes some beautiful stamps commemorating historical events, special people, flora and fauna, and much more. But these only come in certain monetary increments so if your invitation is an odd size or weight, you may need to use more than one. A fabulous new alternative is to make custom stamps online. These cost slightly more than regular postage, but you can create a stamp for the specific thickness, size, and weight of each invitation, as well as design the image. I recently hosted a tea where I agonized over the invitation design. I even used a custom color for the ink. After all of that effort, I found out I would have had to put three stamps on the envelope. Instead, I designed a stamp with an image that recalled the floral illustration on the invitation in a color that echoed the special ink.*

HONORING

CAROLYNE ROEHM
LAUNCHING HER NEW BOOK
A Passion for Blue and White
AND

LISA NEWSOM
EDITOR-IN-CHIEF
Veranda Magazine

PLEASE JOIN US FOR TEA
AND AN INFORMAL TALK
WEDNESDAY, THE FIFTH OF NOVEMBER
AT FOUR O'CLOCK IN THE AFTERNOON

JOE NYE NEW YORK
AT CLAREMONT · ART AND DESIGN BUILDING
1293 THIRD AVENUE · NEW YORK

R.S.V.P.
CHRISTINA JUAREZ 212.355.7127

These beautiful letterpress invitations were for a tea I hosted in New York. Dauphine Press custom-colored the ink and created a special stamp that matched the invitation.

PROOFING

Proofread the invitations yourself and, if possible, have someone else look them over, too.

■ *Get a proof of anything that you are having printed—always. Even if you've seen something that is very similar in a paper store or on a computer screen, you'll never know what your invitation is going to look like until you see a proof.*

■ *Have at least ten percent more invitations and envelopes than the number of guests you are planning for, to account for errors in addressing and filling in, and changes in the guest list.*

■ *Take the stuffed envelope to the post office to check how much postage you'll need. It's worth the extra trip on the front end to save you the*

aggravation of having all the invitations returned with an ugly sticker on the front that reads "Insufficient Postage"!

■ *Double-check zip codes and make sure they are legible.*

■ *Spell out all words in both the address and the return address—don't use abbreviations. I know this takes extra effort, but the overall effect of a well-addressed envelope reflects the care you are putting into the event. The one exception I make is that if you live in Los Angeles or New York City, it's okay to write LA or NYC on a very informal invitation.*

Visit us registered at

George, Beverly Hills

Tiffany & Co.

Williams~Sonoma

...month of April

...o'clock in the afternoon

The Peninsula Beverly Hills

Miss Elizabeth...

Mr. Joseph Nye

9239 DOHENY ROAD
WEST HOLLYWOOD, CALIFORNIA 90069

A NYE F...

JOE,

IN CELEBRATION OF HIS ...
THURSDAY, JUNE 30 THROUGH SUNDAY, JULY 3

THE BROADMOOR
COLORADO SPRING...

PLEASE REPLY BY JUNE 1ST

...E JOIN US
...NUAL PICNI...
...LY 4TH
...MIDNIGHT
... FAMILY
...68TH STREET
...NSAS CITY

Chris 50th
Kindly respond by August 28th

M _____

_____ will attend

_____ unable to attend

...Sunday celebration
for *Chris 50th*
...lasting Dinner and Dancing
...rday, the ninth of September
Six o'clock in the evening
Bel Air C...

Joe Nye and Will...
invite you for
A Sunday Celebration
Sunday, the fourteenth of November
twelve noon
The Valley Hunt Club
520 South Orange Grove Boulevard
Pasadena
Please reply
626 · 653·3100

Mr. Nye

AT THE EVENT

At some gatherings, the paper element will continue at the party itself, in the form of place cards, menu cards, or even name tags and favors. Your design choices for these party elements, which you can have custom printed or make yourself, should relate to your invitations; as with invitations, the design and type of printing should reflect the kind of gathering you are having. With these party elements, however, you'll also want to think a little more about the flowers, the table settings, and the rest of the decor.

Menus and place cards are customary for formal gatherings but can fit nicely at more casual ones as well. A square of colored paper stock with the menu items written in a bold, contrasting color, for instance, is an unexpected touch that guests will undoubtedly appreciate, even if the meal is served as a buffet. And no matter how laid-back the mood is, seeing their names printed on cards by the entry or by their place settings will always make your guests feel special and welcome. Your guests are likely to take these pieces home as souvenirs of the event, especially if they feel you made the gesture just for them.

Above all, let the spirit of your party guide your choices, and don't be afraid of making bad ones. When it comes to the paper elements, there are no mistakes—at least none that can't be avoided by a little proofreading.

For an inexpensive way to dress up a place setting, lay a single flower on the napkin.

CONNOR

Above: **For a dressy dinner party, place cards really dignify the table.** *Opposite:* **A seating chart will help you make sure that you're assembling the right mix of guests at the table.**

Below and right: Store-bought ribbon and a hand-tied bow are the finishing touches on inexpensive, glossy pink bags filled with party favors—a festive touch and a souvenir guests can take home.

Opposite: A huge bouquet of pink carnations and favors lined up at the entrance to your party are sure to excite your guests.

FLOWERS

FLOWERS

You and your party should direct the flowers, not the other way around. It's natural to be tempted by the luscious varieties you see at flower shops and flower markets, but remember: The effect of flowers is not only in the surprise of seeing an unusual variety or a particularly vibrant color but also in how they have been arranged. The most powerful arrangement is often one in which common flowers have been used in an unexpected way. So let your choices be guided by what's fresh, natural, and easy to work with, and most importantly, by what you like!

These sweet peas are for an intimate spring lunch.

SOURCING

Flowers seem to be available everywhere these days. My favorite place to shop for flowers is near my house at a high-end grocery store that has beautiful blooms at remarkably affordable prices. If you live in a city, flower markets are another wonderful option. They are typically open to the public during the day, after certain "trade only" hours. The bounty and choice at a flower market is unrivaled; a trip to the market can be overwhelming, but the sheer volume of flowers you'll see there will be a wonderful source of inspiration. Of course, there's absolutely nothing wrong with going the traditional route and buying your flowers from a florist.

Part of the thrill and the beauty of flowers is their impermanence and their ability to evoke specific seasons and moods. I suggest choosing your flowers as you would choose produce in a farmer's market: with an eye to what is best at that particular time of year. In the spring, people want asparagus, not root vegetables. Consider your flowers in the same way.

Shopping your grocery store or flower market is a great way to get more flowers for your money.

SELECTION

Decorating with flowers is like cooking: Once you have a certain recipe mastered, you'll want to go back to it again and again. I have several staple flowers that I use all the time. Carnations, for instance, are one of my favorites for parties. They remind me of one of my favorite movies of all time *Auntie Mame*. The film is worth renting just to see the flower arrangements! Carnations also have a starring role in the Cecil Beaton—designed credits for *My Fair Lady*. Carnations are sometimes thought of as being out of fashion, but that's exactly why I like to use them: They're unexpected! They're also inexpensive, last forever, and can be arranged effortlessly. What more could you ask for from a flower? Take the entire bunch in your hand, trim all the stems across at once, throw the bouquet into your favorite cachepot, and your centerpiece is done! My favorites are the red and pink ones. Sometimes I'll use the wonderful ivory

variety—but I draw the line at blue and green.

It's fun to try new things, and there will, of course, be occasions when your favorite flowers won't quite do. But don't be afraid to come back to your standbys. You can adapt the presentation to different settings, and in time, these will become part of a signature look.

The specifics of the party should also guide your choice of flowers. A formal event will look more pulled together if you use just one type of flower, but for more casual gatherings, you can convey a sense of fun with a mixed bouquet. If the party has a theme, consider the flowers not only as part of the color scheme, but also as a way to set the mood. For an island-themed party, for instance, I like to use tropical blooms such as

A centerpiece of all the same kind of flower is elegant and easy.

torch ginger and bird-of-paradise. If you are celebrating a holiday, it, too, can offer some cues. Shamrock plants (*Oxalis regnellii*) are wonderful at a St. Patrick's Day brunch. For the Fourth of July, red geraniums in blue-and-white jardinieres are festive and patriotic. If there isn't an obvious floral connection between your theme and your party, brainstorm or look online.

If your party doesn't have a theme, other details—such as the menu, the table setting, how the food will be served, and the level of formality—should guide your choices of flowers. Peonies will complement a Sunday roast served on good china, while dendrobium orchids work well with bamboo tableware at a sophisticated, Asian-inspired cocktail party. If you are having a sit-down meal, you'll want a centerpiece that isn't higher than 9 or 10 inches so as not to obstruct your guests' views across the table; but if you are having a buffet, you can use taller, looser arrangements. Flowers can also help convey the tone: Roses, for example, are more formal than daisies.

It used to be that many flowers were only available in specific seasons; now, like fruits and vegetables, most flowers are available year-round—for better and for worse. Some flowers still evoke the essence of the particular time of year in which they traditionally peak. But now that flowers are grown and shipped from all over the world, those flowers that signaled the arrival of a certain season are in continuous supply, so their "specialness" doesn't seem as special when they are used at other times of the year. Additionally, there is something that may ring false or seem incongruous about using flowers out of their natural season. (I don't think I'll ever think of anything besides spring when I see lilacs, peonies, and tulips in full regalia!)

Use flowers that are really fresh, in season, and appropriate for the time of the year you're having your party.

PRESENTATION

Single stems and demure bouquets look lovely on printed cards or as gifts, but you achieve drama in flowers by using them in multitudes. For parties, instead of spending a lot of money on a few stems of expensive varieties, I buy more stems of less expensive flowers. In this case, quantity is quality. For a typical 6-inch-diameter cachepot, for instance, you are going to need at least three bunches. (Flowers are typically sold in bunches of ten or twenty-five stems.) If you use Oasis floral foam, you will require fewer flowers.

In arrangements of a single variety, uniformity conveys elegance; on the other hand, when creating a mixed bouquet, I like to emphasize contrast in color, shape, and texture as much as possible. If you are using two kinds of flowers, try pairing something lacy such as mimosa with something substantial (tulips, perhaps) to give the arrangement visual contrast.

For a beachy summer supper, try mixing an exotic flower such as orchids with a spicier one such as gerbera daisies. In a mixed bouquet, you can use as many species as you like; the more types of flowers you incorporate, the more casual and effortless the arrangement will appear.

Flower aficionados are always trying to think of things to put flowers in besides regular vases. I put flowers in family heirlooms; in mason jars and other glassware; or in galvanized steel buckets. If I'm throwing a party in the fall, I like to hollow out a pumpkin and put flowers into it. Thinking "outside the vase" is great, but when you are hunting for something original to put your flowers in, it's good to have those plastic liners handy.

Don't ever put flowers into a metal container without a liner. It's not good for the flowers, and water may stain the inside of your vessel. The same goes for antique containers of any material—they may not be watertight and could easily be damaged.

A mixture of hot colors makes
for a fun and informal look.

*Gypsophila, dreaded
by many, is wonderful
when used alone.
It's easy to work with,
inexpensive, and different.*

CONTAINERS

■ *A soup tureen with the lid removed is a perfect container for a classic low-and-round centerpiece for a round table. (Use Oasis floral foam to secure the flowers.)*

■ *If you've inherited a silver coffee service, you can use it at a party in a less dowdy way by opening or removing the lids of all the pieces and throwing red carnations into them.*

■ *Mint julep cups can be gotten for practically nothing these days, and they look lovely filled with flowers. Place a single arrangement as an accent in the powder room, or use them in profusion down the center of a long table.*

■ *A simple idea, but always a crowd-pleaser: Place flowers in a clear glass, cylindrical vase.*

■ *Flowers look very pretty in ordinary water pitchers. I have one of my grandmother's that is lettuce-green thumbprint glass and looks lovely filled with pink carnations or tulips.*

■ *Wicker baskets are very charming. One thing I often do is get a big bunch of baby's breath, trim and separate the stems, and place the bouquet, without water, into a wicker basket. Yes, that's right—without water. Flowers don't last forever, no matter what you do; if you let yourself get caught up in trying to keep them alive for as long as possible, you'll miss out on a lot of fun.*

■ *Find some antique celery vases at a secondhand shop or an estate sale. Their shape makes them really easy to arrange flowers in. A humble-seeming cluster of three—all of different heights—will be more than the sum of its parts and always look surprisingly grand. It's okay— better even—if the vases don't match. (A good rule of thumb for any design situation is that odd numbers are better than even.)*

■ *Old-fashioned terracotta pots and saucers are a natural base for garden arrangements.*

■ *A vintage silver ice bucket (it doesn't matter if it comes from Tiffany or a secondhand shop) is a perfect container for a blooming plant such as an azalea. Or you can toss several bunches of roses into it for a quick, casual, but grand-looking gesture. Very Ralph Lauren.*

Fruit in a bowl can be fast
to assemble, pretty, and
inexpensive in lieu of flowers.

PREPARATION

I think that the best flowers for a party are the ones that are the easiest to work with. Flowers should serve the event, not the other way around. In the hours before company arrives, there are many better tasks to devote time to than fighting with your flowers to get them just so. For a gathering, pick varieties that you won't have to struggle with.

Longevity is a factor when you are buying flowers that you want to last through the week; but when you are buying them for a specific event, your main concern should be that what you choose is at their peak at the party. If you get a few extra days out of them, consider that a bonus. Unopened blossoms typically take between three and five days to open. Once open, most flowers stay fresh for another twenty-four to forty-eight hours. So time your shopping trip around the day of the party, and then choose your flowers accordingly. When you are at the flower store or market, pinch the leaves to see if the flowers are fresh. They should feel firm and crisp.

TOOLS TO HAVE ON HAND

- *Sharp knife only used for flowers*

- *Good scissors*

- *Garden clippers*

- *Oasis floral foam (to hold the stems in place in shallow containers and to deliver moisture)*

- *Sturdy plastic liners (slip these into antiques and other containers that aren't watertight)*

- *Mint julep cups, baby cups, or other small decorative cups that can hold a few blossoms (to place in the powder room)*

MY FAVORITE FLOWERS FOR PARTIES

Bunches of carnations, alstroemeria, chrysanthemums, and gerbera daisies are often available at the grocery store.

SUNFLOWER

ORCHID

YARROW

FUJI MUM

"CONNECTICUT
KING" LILY

GARDEN ROSE

ALSTROEMERIA

GLADIOLUS

VIBURNUM

STATICE

IRIS

HYDRANGEA

GYPSOPHILA

HYDRANGEA

CALLA LILY

GARDENIA

GARDEN ROSE

ORCHID

HYDRANGEA

CARNATION

LARKSPUR

RANUNCULUS

DAHLIA

GERBERA DAISY

145 FLAIR

ESSENTIALS

ENTRYWAY, CLOSET AND POWDER ROOM

I f you have an entrance hall where you will greet guests, it's nice to put something special there for the party: a bouquet of fresh flowers, a stack of "take-me-homes," or a burning candle. If you have a foyer table of some kind, you can set any or all of these things on it.

If you don't have a coat closet, you should place guests' coats in a bedroom. If you have the room, clear out another closet (so visitors don't feel as though they are invading a personal space) and buy good-quality, uniform hangers on which to hang coats.

Don't forget your powder room. As with the touches in the entryway, fresh flowers, a scented candle, and proper guest towels signify that the powder room has been specially prepared for the gathering, a thoughtful attention to detail that is bound to be appreciated by your guests.

A big bouquet of gypsophila, along with an elegant party favor, greets guests in a client's entrance hall.

Above: **Nice quality paper guest towels are okay. Place a shell on top to hold them in place.** *Opposite:* **A tiny bouquet of yellow freesia and green hydrangea sit on the edge of the powder-room sink.**

CANDLES AND LIGHTING

Ambience can make or break a party. Lighting, along with decor and flowers, convey the party mood. And because it's not practical to install new lightbulbs every time you have company, candles are an easy and elegant way to create the ambience you desire.

Taper candles (the long skinny ones) in black or cream are good to keep on hand. They add a simple, romantic twinkle to the table and go with everything. I also like to scatter small votives around a table or put one at each place setting. When I want a dramatic effect, I set candlesticks in large hurricane shades and place those on the table as well. Once dinner is served, I remove them so that they don't obstruct the view across the table.

Always light your candles in advance of the party to make sure the wicks are in working order. Also, it is considered gauche to have an unlit candle in view. If you decorate with candles, don't forget to light them!

These are the tools of the trade: tapered candles in black and cream, and glass bobeches to protect your table.

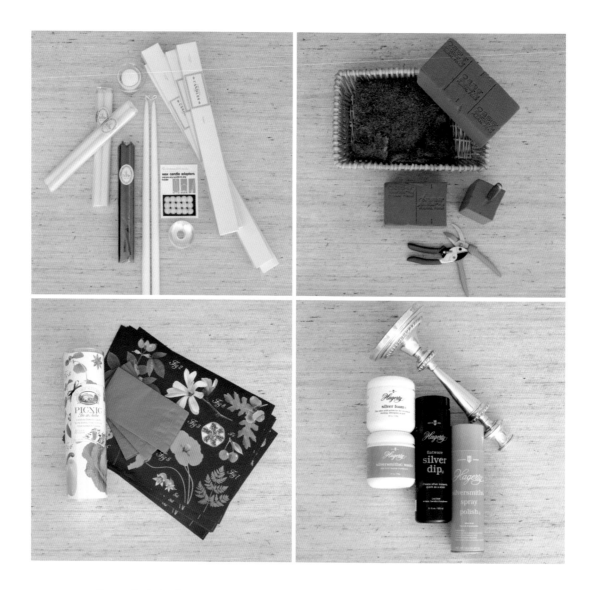

Above, clockwise from top left: **More tools of the trade: tapered candles, floral foam and the right clippers, silver cleaners and polishes to make the job easier, paper placemats and napkins for a quick breakfast or lunch.** *Opposite:* **A dense, made-to-order table pad and "silencing" cloth over the pad.**

MY MUST-HAVES

■ *12- or 15-inch taper candles in black and cream. I like cream for spring and summer and black for fall and winter, but I always have both on hand.*

■ *Bobeches. Slip these around the base of the tapers to keep wax from dripping all over the tablecloth or dining table.*

■ *Tablepad. This extra layer of padding will protect your table from heat. It may have to be custom-made, but I think it's worth the expense. (Check your phone directory or online to locate a company that will come over to make a template of your table.)*

■ *Silencing cloth. This felt cloth is custom cut to fit your table and goes underneath your tablecloth. It's a nice touch that seems to have gone out of fashion, but I consider it a must. It softens the edge of your table and buffers sound so the clanging of glasses and plates don't spoil a dinner. You use the silencing cloth over the dense, hard table pad.*

CLEANING THE SILVER

Water is an enemy of silver and is, in fact, one cause of tarnishing.

■ As mentioned earlier, if you use your silver often, it won't need to be polished regularly. However, whenever you use a piece of silver, make sure it is polished—nothing is uglier than tarnished silver.

■ If you're in real trouble, there is a product that you can dip your silver into that literally strips the tarnish right off of it. You must polish the piece immediately after dipping it to remove the chemicals and to restore its original sheen.

■ I always wash anything that's going to touch food with dishwashing liquid after polishing, just to ensure that the polish and everything else has been removed. (If it's a candelabra or something decorative, I don't even rinse it, because the silver polish is more effective if the item doesn't get wet.) After polishing, use super-hot water to rinse your piece, and then dry it thoroughly.

RESOURCE GUIDE

Agraria
1123 Lillian Way
Los Angeles, CA 90038
800.824.3632
323.462.7898
www.agrariahome.com
custsvc@agrariahome.com

Charlotte Moss
212.308.7088
www.charlottemoss.com
info@charlottemoss.com

Classic Party Rentals
11766 Wilshire Blvd., Suite 350
Los Angeles, CA 90025
310.535.3660
www.classicpartyrentals.com
infola@classicpartyrentals.com

Crate & Barrel
438 North Beverly Drive
Beverly Hills, CA 90210
800.967.6696
www.crateandbarrel.com

Creative Candles
800.237.9711
816.474.9711
www.creativecandles.com
mail@creativecandles.com

Dauphine Press
888.869.0659
707.776.0790
www.dauphinepress.com

Deborah Sears
Isis Ceramics Ltd.
The New Toffee Factory
West Hill Farm
Church Lane
Horton-cum-Studley
Oxford, OX33 1AP
England
+44 (0)18 65 35 80 00
www.isisceramics.com
sales@isisceramics.com

Geary's Beverly Hills
351 North Beverly Drive
Beverly Hills, CA 90210
310.273.4741

Gelson's
8330 West Santa Monica Boulevard
West Hollywood, CA 90069
323.656.5580
www.gelsons.com

Gracious Style
888.828.7170
www.graciousstyle.com

Hagerty
800.348.5162
www.hagertyusa.com
info@hagertyusa.com

Hilary Williams Calligraphy
818.760.3406
www.hil-ink.com
hilary@hil-ink.com

Hollyhock
817 Hilldale Avenue
West Hollywood, CA 90069
310.777.0100
www.hollyhockinc.com

Julep Custom Florals
323.466.7292
www.julepstudio.com
sabrina@julepstudio.com

Juliska
46 Canal Street
Stamford, CT 06902
888.414.8448
203.316.0212
www.juliska.com
info.@juliska.com

Knorr Candle Shop
14906 Via de La Valle
Del Mar, CA 92014
800.807.2337
858.755.2051
www.knorrbeeswax.com

Koontz Hardware
8914 Santa Monica Boulevard
West Hollywood, CA 90069
310.652.0123
www.koontz.com

Landis Gifts & Stationery
138 North Larchmont Boulevard
Los Angeles, CA 90004
323.465.7003
www.landisgiftsandstationery.com
info@landisgiftsandstationery.com

Los Angeles Flower District
766 Wall Street
Los Angeles, CA 90014
213.627.3696
ww.laflowerdistrict.com

L.A. Table Pad Co.
866.528.2253
661.263.9289
www.latablepad.com
emailus@latable.com

Lunt Silversmiths
800.242.2774
www.luntsilver.com
webquestions@luntsilver.com

Nancy Stanley Waud
8918 Burton Way, Suite 4
Beverly Hills, CA 90211
310.273.3690
By appointment to the trade
www.nancystanleywaud.com
nswfinelinens@gmail.com

Odd Balls
800.541.0174
www.oddballsinvitations.net
comments@oddballsinvitations.net

Paul Marra Design
868 North La Cienega Boulevard
Los Angeles, CA 90069
310.659.8190
www.paulmarradesign.com
paulmarradesign@sbcglobal.net

Pickard China
847.395.3800
www.pickardchina.com
info@pickardchina.com

Soolip Paperie & Press
8646 Melrose Avenue
West Hollywood, CA 90069
310.360.0545
www.soolip.com
paperie@soolip.com

Uniquities
323.651.5596
www.uniquities-sales.com
uniquit11@aol.com

Williams Sonoma Home
888.922.4108
www.wshome.com

Zimmer + Rohde
+49 (0)61 71 76 32 02
www.zimmer-rohde.com
info@zimmer-rohde.com

First published in the United States of America
in 2010
by Rizzoli International Publications, Inc.
300 Park Avenue South, New York, NY 10010
www.rizzoliusa.com

Designed by Doug Turshen
Sandy Gilbert, Rizzoli Editor
Ellen R. Cohen, Rizzoli Production Editor

ISBN: 978-0-8478-3317-7
Library of Congress Control Number: 2009942352

Printed in China

2010 2011 2012 2013 2014 / 10 9 8 7 6 5 4 3 2 1